RSPB first book of
butterflies and moths

Derek Niemann

D0319132

A & C BLACK
AN IMPRINT OF BLOOMSBURY
LONDON NEW DELHI NEW YORK SYDNEY

Published 2012 by A&C Black,
An imprint of Bloomsbury Publishing Plc
50 Bedford Square, London WC1B 3DP
www.bloomsbury.com

ISBN: 978-1-4081-6572-0

Printed in China by C & C Offset Printing Co., Ltd.

A&C Black uses paper produced from elemental
chlorine-free pulp, harvested from managed
sustainable forests.

10 9 8 7 6 5 4 3 2

Contents

Butterflies and moths

Butterflies and moths come in lots of colours – red, blue, green, yellow, orange. Be careful not to touch them though. Their wings and bodies are very soft.

This book will help you name many of the butterflies and moths you see. It tells you where you might find them. And it shows you how you can tell them apart.

At the back of this book is a Spotter's Guide to help you remember the butterflies and moths you find. Tick them off as you spot them. You can also find out more about the life of a butterfly here.

Turn the page to find out more about butterflies and moths!

Large skipper

Skippers get their name from the way they skip from flower to flower. You can see these butterflies in places where there is long grass. Skipper caterpillars like to eat the grass.

Skippers often sit with their front wings lifted up and their back wings down flat.

Orange and brown wings

Skipper caterpillars have a flap on their bottom for flicking away their poo!

Swallowtail

This is the biggest butterfly in Britain. It has very long tips on its wings that look like a swallow's tail. You can only find this butterfly in a marshy area called the Norfolk Broads.

The female lays her eggs on a plant called milk parsley.

Yellow and black wings

Blue and red patches that look like eyes

Long tips on back wings

Brimstone

Look for this yellow butterfly in gardens, woods and fields in early spring. This insect is the colour of butter. That may be where the word butterfly comes from.

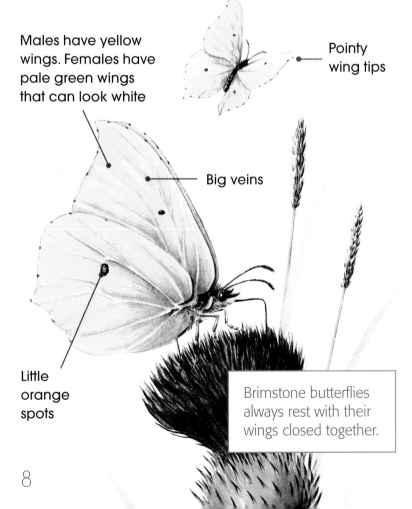

Males have yellow wings. Females have pale green wings that can look white

Pointy wing tips

Big veins

Little orange spots

Brimstone butterflies always rest with their wings closed together.

Large white

This butterfly is one of two called a cabbage white. The caterpillars eat cabbages and brussel sprouts.

In autumn, the caterpillar turns into a cocoon called a chrysalis [kriss-ah-liss]. It hatches as a butterfly in the spring.

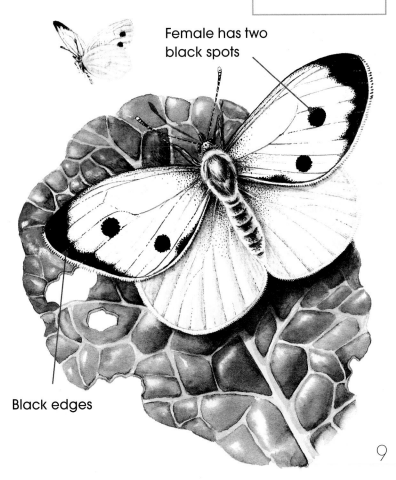

Female has two black spots

Black edges

Small white

This butterfly is also sometimes called a cabbage white. Small whites have long tongues to drink nectar. They roll them up when they do not need them.

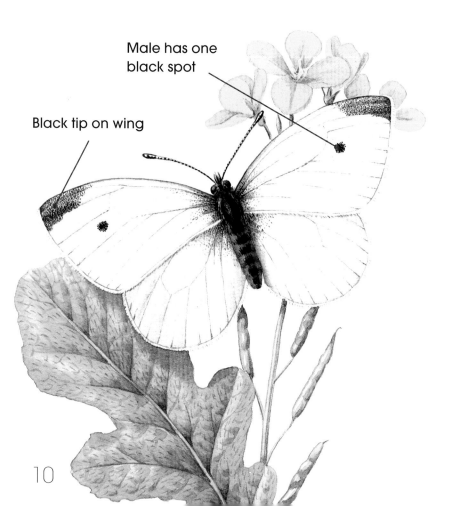

Male has one black spot

Black tip on wing

Green-veined white

Look for this white butterfly in the countryside, especially in damp places. When it lands, you can see the big green veins on its wings.

Green streaks on underside of wing

Female butterflies only eat nectar. Males sometimes land on bare earth to lick up goodness in the soil.

Female has more dark marks than male

Orange-tip

This is the only white butterfly
that has orange tips on its wings.
Orange-tips fly in May and June.
Look for them in fields and at
the sides of the road.

Only the males have orange
tips. The females have
wings with black edges.

Orange
tip

White

Undersides have
patches of green
that look like moss.

Purple hairstreak

Purple hairstreaks don't fly very often! Most of the time, they sit in trees, licking sticky honeydew off the leaves.

Sometimes purple hairstreaks come down to drink nectar from bramble flowers.

Silver underneath with white streak

Purple above

This butterfly gets its name from the streak on the underside of its wings.

Small copper

You can see this little orange
and brown butterfly all over
Britain. Watch it fly up from its
perch to chase another butterfly
away. This is my place!

Sits with wings
open to catch
the sun

Black spots

The small copper
caterpillars feed on
plants called docks
and sorrels.

Back wings
mostly brown

Brown argus

There are two kinds of argus butterfly that look very similar. In southern Britain, you usually see brown argus butterflies. Northern brown argus butterflies live in places with lots of hills.

This is a brown argus. A Northern brown argus does not usually have orange spots on its front wings.

Dark brown

Rows of orange spots on edges of wings

Black spot. Often a white spot on northern brown argus

Common blue

The common blue butterfly lives in grassy places in the countryside. But only the male is blue. The female is mostly brown.

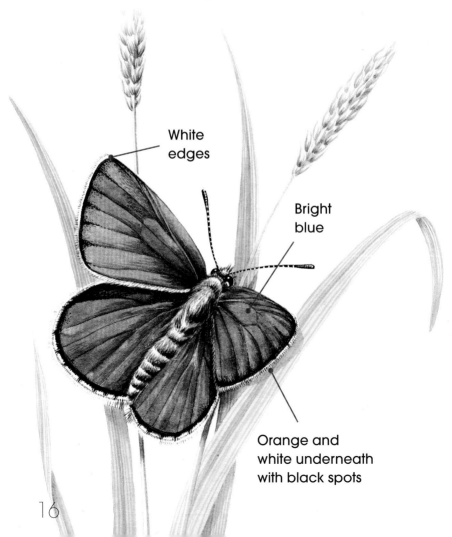

White edges

Bright blue

Orange and white underneath with black spots

Holly blue

Look out for this blue butterfly in gardens, even in the middle of cities. It flutters around trees and bushes.

Caterpillars that hatch in spring eat holly berries, buds and leaves.

Pale blue with black spots underneath

Bright blue

Caterpillars that hatch in summer eat ivy leaves.

Painted lady

Every spring, these butterflies
fly all the way here from
North Africa. They can fly
over 100 miles in a day.

White marks on black tips

Wings slightly
pointed

This insect was named
because it was supposed
to look like a grand lady
wearing lots of make-up!

Orangey-brown

Small tortoiseshell

These common butterflies like to travel. Every day, they fly from place to place. In the autumn, the adults sleep in sheds, garages, or even in people's houses.

Small tortoiseshell caterpillars make a web around themselves. It hides them from creatures that want to eat them.

Orange and black

Blue spots

Red admiral

In spring or autumn, this big, strong butterfly flies hundreds of miles to get here from other countries. The adults feed on nectar and rotting fruit in our gardens.

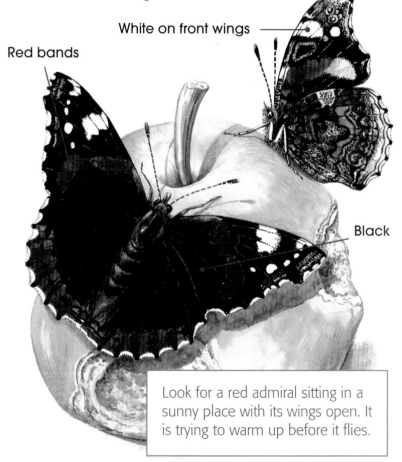

White on front wings

Red bands

Black

Look for a red admiral sitting in a sunny place with its wings open. It is trying to warm up before it flies.

Peacock

The big eyes on this butterfly's wings look just like the eyes in a peacock's tail. They are not real eyes, of course!

Look out for spiky black peacock caterpillars feeding on nettles.

Black markings

Big eye shape on each wing

Red wings

Comma

This butterfly wanders through the countryside looking for places to feed and breed. When it closes its wings together, it looks just like a dead leaf.

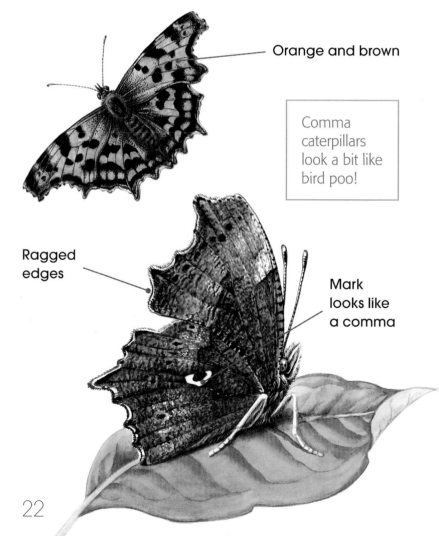

Orange and brown

Comma caterpillars look a bit like bird poo!

Ragged edges

Mark looks like a comma

Dark green fritillary

These butterflies are orange with lots of brown spots. There are lots of different kinds of fritillary.

Fritillaries lay their eggs on violet plants.

Silver spots

Orange with brown streaks and spots

Speckled wood

A male speckled wood lands in the hedge. When another insect comes close, he flies up to it. If it is another male speckled wood, he will try to chase it away.

The caterpillars can live through the winter on the ground. They eat grass.

Dark brown

Black and white eye shapes

Creamy speckles

Gatekeeper

This butterfly is also called the hedge brown. You can see it flying over the long grass at the bottom of hedges, and at the edges of fields.

We only see these butterflies in July and August.

Eyespot with two white spots

Orange

Brown streaks on front wings (male)

Tiny white spots on back wings

Brown

Marbled white

You can always pick out a marbled white. Look for this black and white butterfly in meadows in July and August.

Females fly over the grass and drop their eggs in it!

White patches on black

Undersides are yellowish

Grayling

Look for graylings flying fast on cliff-tops by the sea. You can also find them in the sand dunes. Some live on heaths and in old quarries too.

After the grayling lands, it tucks its front wings under its back wings. This makes it very hard to see.

Front wings are orange and brown

Underside is grey and white

Meadow brown

You will see lots of meadow browns in the countryside. Like many butterflies, it has only four legs that work. It has two shorter front legs. They don't seem to do anything useful.

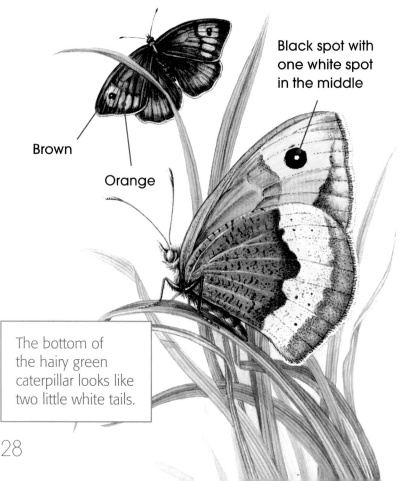

Black spot with one white spot in the middle

Brown

Orange

The bottom of the hairy green caterpillar looks like two little white tails.

Ringlet

This dark butterfly lives in damp, grassy places. Look for it in woodland. Unlike most butterflies, it can fly when it is cool and even when it is raining.

When it is scared by a bird, the caterpillar drops off the grass to the ground below.

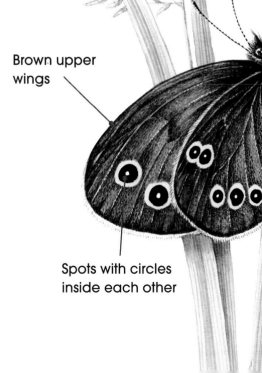

Brown upper wings

Spots with circles inside each other

Small heath

This tiny butterfly is not easy to see. It flies very close to the ground and lands with its wings closed. It lives in places that have long grass.

Eye spot

Orangey-brown

Grey, brown and white bands on underside of lower wing

Males live for only a week and spend most of their short lives looking for a mate.

Burnet moth

Unlike most moths, burnet moths fly during the day. They don't fly very far or very fast. Look for them in summer, fluttering about in long grass.

Red is for danger! Burnet moths are poisonous so birds don't eat them.

Red spots

Black

Thin wings

Cinnabar moth

This moth flies in the day and night in grassy places. You are more likely to see its orange and black caterpillars. They sit out in the open on ragwort and groundsel flowers.

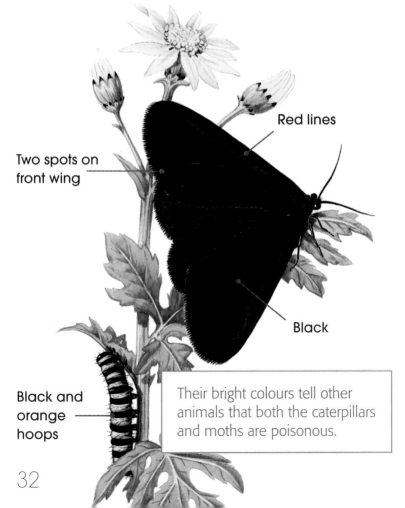

Red lines

Two spots on front wing

Black

Black and orange hoops

Their bright colours tell other animals that both the caterpillars and moths are poisonous.

Poplar hawkmoth

Don't be scared by this huge moth coming to your window at night. Like all moths, it is harmless. The moth is attracted to lights.

Back wings tucked under front wings

Brown colours match the tree trunks it sits on

This moth scares off birds and mammals by showing them the red on its back wings.

Hummingbird hawkmoth

This big moth beats its wings so fast they are hard to see. It flies up to a flower and hovers over it. Then it sticks its long tongue in to drink the nectar.

Long black tongue

Orange on back wings

Black and white marks on body

Wings beat very fast

People often mistake this moth for a hummingbird. But those tiny birds live in America.

Elephant hawkmoth

This moth is named after its caterpillar. People say it looks like an elephant's trunk! The moth comes out at night and drinks nectar from honeysuckle.

When it is scared, the caterpillar tucks its head back into its body. Do you think it looks like a trunk?

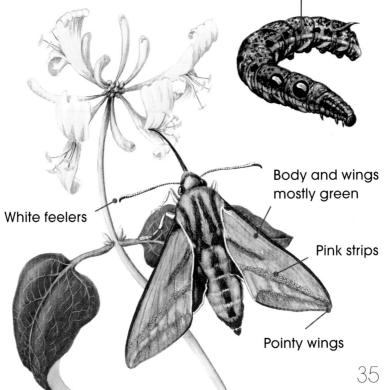

Caterpillar

Body and wings mostly green

White feelers

Pink strips

Pointy wings

Large yellow underwing moth

Underwing moths rest on a tree trunk or the stem of a plant. They are very hard to see there. If something disturbs them, they lift their front wings. Then you can see their colourful back wings.

Birds are surprised when this moth shows its colourful back wings. This gives it time to escape.

Brown or grey front wings with a pattern like tree bark

Bright yellow back wings

Black dot on wing tip

Brimstone moth

You can see this yellow moth in summer and autumn. It is attracted to light at night. The caterpillars feed on the leaves of trees and bushes.

In the south, brimstones can lay eggs three times in a year.

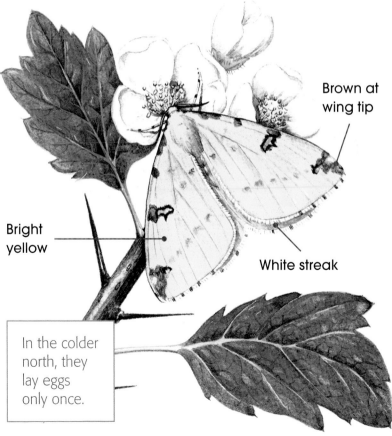

Brown at wing tip

Bright yellow

White streak

In the colder north, they lay eggs only once.

Buff-tip moth

This moth rests on a tree with its wings closed. Hungry birds think it is just a broken twig. It is a great way for the buff-tip to hide during the day.

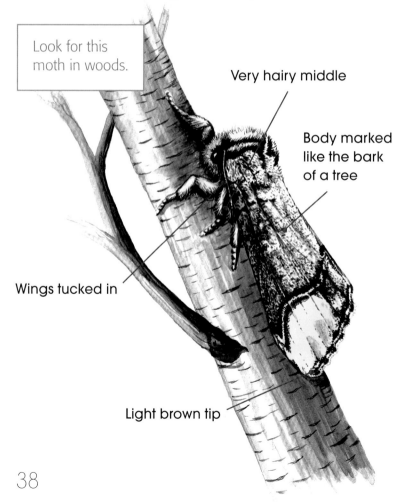

Look for this moth in woods.

Very hairy middle

Body marked like the bark of a tree

Wings tucked in

Light brown tip

Angle shades moth

This moth looks a bit like a dead leaf! Its wings are lots of different green and brown colours. They look dry and crinkly.

The caterpillar digs into the soil in the autumn and makes a cocoon for itself.

This triangle is green and pink at first. It soon turns brown.

Wing looks as if it has folds

Long wing tips

Silver Y moth

The little silvery white Y marks on its wings give this moth its name. Look for silver Y moths in the garden just as it is getting dark. They are searching for flower nectar.

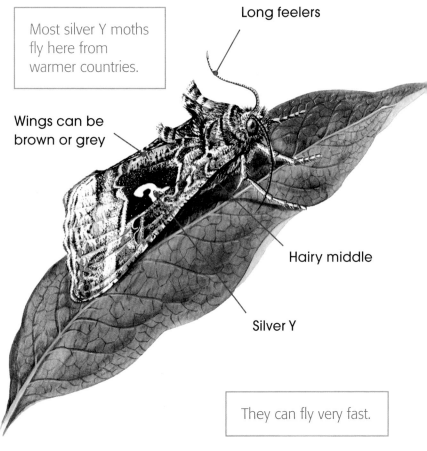

Most silver Y moths fly here from warmer countries.

Long feelers

Wings can be brown or grey

Hairy middle

Silver Y

They can fly very fast.

The life of a butterfly

The female butterfly lays her eggs. Caterpillars hatch from the eggs.

When a caterpillar has grown big enough, its skin hardens and changes shape into a chrysalis (kriss-ah-liss). Some caterpillars also spin a cocoon around themselves.

The caterpillar turns into a butterfly inside the chrysalis. The chrysalis then opens up and the butterfly flies away.

Useful words

cocoon a cover that an insect wraps around itself for protection

nectar the sweet liquid that flowers make to attract insects

Spotter's guide

How many of these butterflies and moths have you seen? Tick them when you spot them.

☐ Large skipper
page 6

☐ Swallowtail
page 7

☐ Brimstone
page 8

☐ Large white
page 9

☐ Small white
page 10

Green-veined white
page 11

Orange-tip
page 12

Purple hairstreak
page 13

Small copper
page 14

Brown argus
page 15

Common blue
page 16

Dark green fritillary
page 23

Speckled wood
page 24

Gatekeeper
page 25

Marbled white
page 26

Grayling
page 27

Meadow brown
page 28

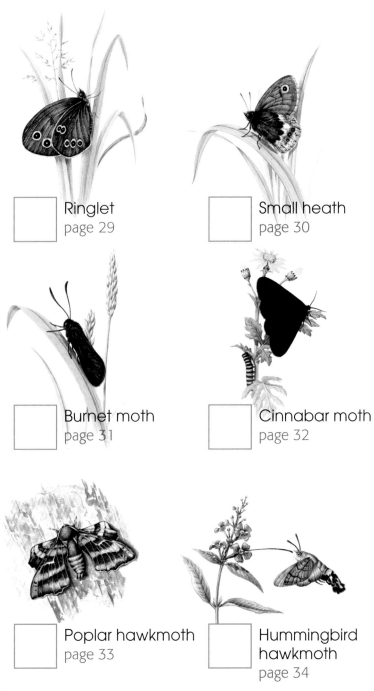

Ringlet
page 29

Small heath
page 30

Burnet moth
page 31

Cinnabar moth
page 32

Poplar hawkmoth
page 33

Hummingbird hawkmoth
page 34

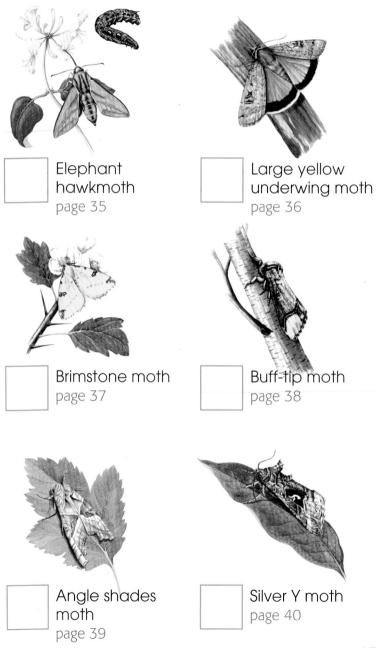

Elephant
hawkmoth

Large yellow
underwing moth

Brimstone moth

Buff-tip moth

Angle shades
moth

Silver Y moth

Find out more

If you have enjoyed this book you might like our club for children. RSPB Wildlife Explorers helps you learn more about nature. You will get a magazine six times a year that tells you all about things you can do.

Visit the world's biggest wildlife club for children at www.rspb.org.uk/youth